THE MAKING OF
MODERN RUSSIA

Library Edition published 1991
Published by Marshall Cavendish Corporation
2415 Jerusalem Avenue
North Bellmore, NY 11710

Typeset by Jamesway Graphics
Hanson Close Middleton Manchester
M24 2HD England

Printed in Spain by Gráficas Reunidas, S. A.

LIBRARY OF CONGRESS
Library of Congress Cataloging-in-Publication
Data

The Making of modern Russia: Peter the
Great, Karl Marx, V.I. Lenin.—Reference ed.
    p. cm—(Exploring the past)
  Includes bibliographical references and
index.
  Summary: Profiles three people who helped
form the Soviet Union: Peter the Great, Karl
Marx, and Vladimir Lenin.
  ISBN 1–85435–416–7
  1. Peter I. Emperor of Russia.
1672-1725—Juvenile literature. 2. Marx, Karl,
1818-1883—Juvenile literature. 3. Lenin,
Vladimir Il'ich, 1870-1924—Juvenile literature.
4. Soviet Union—Kings and
rulers—Biography—Juvenile literature. 5.
Communists—Biography—Juvenile literature.
6. Soviet Union—History—Juvenile literature.
[1. Peter I. Emperor of Russia. 1672-1725. 2.
Marx, Karl, 1818-1883. Lenin, Vladimir Il'ich,
1870-1924. 4. Kings, queens, rulers, etc. 5.
Communists. 6. Soviet Union—History.]
I. Marshall Cavendish Corporation. II. Series.
DK37,6.M34 1991
947′,00992—dc20
[B]   91-16350
                                                      CIP
                                                       AC

ISBN 1–85435–411–6 (Set)
ISBN 1–85435–416–7 (Volume 5)

The Making of Modern Russia is number five in
Exploring the Past II series.

Credits: Front cover Richard Schollins; page 1
Lauros-Giraudon; page 3 Jean Loup Charmet

THE MAKING OF
MODERN RUSSIA

Peter the Great

Karl Marx

V.I. Lenin

Marshall Cavendish Corporation

NEW YORK · TORONTO · LONDON · SYDNEY · SINGAPORE

STAFF LIST

Series editor

Jenny Mulherin

Assistant editors

Ray Granger
Neil Harris
Rick Morris

Art editor

Frank Cawley

Assistant art editor

Sue Downing

Designer

Kevin Humphrey

Production controller

Inger Faulkner

Managing editor

Maggie Calmels

Michael Holford

Titles in EXPLORING THE PAST Series

The French Revolution
Marie Antoinette
Lord Nelson
Napoleon Bonaparte

The Making of America
George Washington
Abraham Lincoln
Buffalo Bill Cody

Giants of the Arts
Ludwig van Beethoven
Charles Dickens
Vincent van Gogh

Giants of Science
Isaac Newton
Charles Darwin
Louis Pasteur

The Making of Modern Russia
Peter the Great
Karl Marx
V.I. Lenin

Twentieth Century Pioneers
The Wright Brothers
Scott of the Antarctic
Neil Armstrong

READER'S GUIDE

Imagine that you owned a time machine, and that you traveled back to the days when your parents were in school. Your hometown and school would look different, while the clothes, music, and magazines that your parents were enjoying might seem odd, perhaps amusing, and certainly "old fashioned" and "out of date". Travel back a few hundred years, and you would be astonished and fascinated by the strange food, homes, even language, of our ancestors.

Time machines do not yet exist, but in this book you can explore one of the most important periods of the past through the eyes of three people who made history happen. An introduction sets the scene and highlights the significant themes of the age, while the chronology lists important events and when they happened to help you to understand the background to the period. There is also a glossary to explain words that you may not understand and a list of other books that you may find useful.

The past is important to us all, for the world we know was formed by the actions of people who inhabited it before us. So, by understanding history, we can better understand the events of our own times. Perhaps that is why you will find exploring the past so exciting, rewarding and fascinating.

Michael Holford

CONTENTS

Richard Schollins

INTRODUCTION

TUC Library

Giancarlo Costa

Today, Russia is one of the most powerful nations in the world. It is also the largest, with a land area of more than eight million square miles. For centuries, though, it was an unorganized collection of tribal states with very little contact with the outside world. From the 13th century, it was effectively isolated from the rest of Europe.

The first stirrings of Russian power came when Ivan the Great, Grand Duke of Muscovy (the area around Moscow) drove out the Mongols and Tartars who were occupying the country at the end of the 16th century. Ivan's grandson, Ivan the Terrible, pushed south from his Moscow base and established an empire that stretched from the Arctic Ocean to the Caspian Sea. This achievement led Ivan the Terrible to be called "Tsar (Emperor) of all the Russias", the first man to hold this illustrious title.

A Feudal Society

Russia was run on strictly feudal lines. The great lords, the boyars, were granted land by the Tsar on condition that they provided him with military help and cash when he needed them; the boyars in turn allowed the peasants, who formed the vast majority of the population, enough land to support themselves in exchange for various services. When the Tsar needed men for his army, the boyars sent their most able-bodied peasants. When he needed money, he raised taxes, and the boyars met his demands by increasing the peasants' rents.

The expansion of Russia required plenty of money, and the first Tsars raised taxes to such a level that the peasants could no longer pay the boyars' rents. They got into debt, and became virtual slaves of the local boyar. Laws were passed preventing them from leaving the lands where they were born to look for somewhere better. This medieval system of serfdom remained more or less intact into the 20th century.

Looking West

Though it was gradually expanding its boundaries to the east, Russia remained largely closed to the rest of Europe until a young idealist, Peter Romanov, replaced his blind, simple-minded half-brother Ivan as Tsar in 1689. Peter looked beyond the borders of his sprawling country, and sought foreign help in creating a navy, an educational system and a more efficient economy. He also introduced heavy industry into a nation that previously relied almost entirely on farming and hunting to support its people.

Perhaps the most far-seeing of Peter's decisions was to

Popperfoto

Bildarchiv Preussicscher Kulturebe-sitz

Roger-Viollet

Novosti

move the Russian capital from Moscow. He built a new city, St. Petersburg, on the Neva river, close to the Baltic Sea. He successfully fought a 21-year war with Sweden for control of the Baltic, allowing his new navy year-round access to the sea. Before this, the only port in Russian control was Archangel, so far north that it was frozen up for much of the year.

Peter was rare among the Tsars of Russia. Most of them left the country no better than they found it, and some considerably worse. The Romanov family, which provided Russia with rulers for 304 years, tended to see

their country only as a way of raising money. They intermarried with foreign royal families and became more and more remote from the mainstream of Russian life.

Through the 19th century, Russia was ruled by a succession of dictatorial Tsars, one of whom, Nicholas I, led his country into war with Britain, France and Turkey in the Crimea in 1854. This war established Russia in the eyes of most of Europe as an uncivilized nation ruled by cruel and vicious men.

Opposition to the Tsar was growing inside Russia, too. Intellectual young Russians took up the ideas of political thinkers in other countries. Some favored Communism, the idea that everyone should work for the government, and that the government should work for the good of everyone. Communism had been introduced to the world in 1848 with the publication of the Communist Manifesto, written by two Germans, Karl Marx and Frederick Engels. Beginning with the stirring words, "Workers of the world unite! You have nothing to lose but your chains!", the Manifesto had a great effect around the world. Other Russians became anarchists, believing that all government was bad, and that no man had the right to tell another what to do. Both groups saw the Tsars as their enemy.

The Last of the Tsars

Nicholas's son, Alexander II, did attempt to improve the farm system and give the peasants a little more freedom. However, he too would not tolerate disagreement, and the feared Tsarist secret police, the Ohkrana, mercilessly hunted down those who opposed him. The only way open to those who wished to reform Russia, it seemed, was violence. Many favored assassination as a way of turning their ideas into reality, and several attempts were made on the life of the Tsars towards the end of the 19th century.

Alexander II was killed by a bomb in 1881. His son,

Alexander III, carried on where his father had left off, sending virtually everyone who disagreed with him to exile in the frozen wastes of Siberia. In 1894, Alexander III died, aged 50, and was succeeded by his son, Nicholas II. Nicholas, just 26 when he came to power, was a gentle, rather weak man, who had almost nothing in common with the people he ruled. Married to a German princess, he spoke English at home and French—for a long time the preferred language of Russian nobles—at court.

Nicholas's wife, Alexandra, though a stronger personality than her husband, was equally blind to the way the vast majority of Russians lived. The royal family led a sheltered, self-indulgent life, spending their summers in a country retreat not far from Moscow and their winters in the Winter Palace in St. Petersburg.

The Roots of Revolution

Nicholas and Alexandra's main concern was the production of a male heir to carry on the Romanov line. Their joy at the birth of their son, Alexei, after three daughters, was spoiled by the discovery that the boy was ill. The only person who seemed able to help him was a low-born monk, Grigor Rasputin, who soon became the most powerful man in the land. Since Nicholas never made his son's illness public, the people were never able to understand Rasputin's power, and it became just another reason to hate the Tsar.

Discontent reached a new height in 1905, after Russia lost a war with Japan. Thousands marched on the Winter Palace, hoping to confront the Tsar with their misery. The Tsar's troops opened fire on them. In the same year, communist and anarchist agitators led strikes, mutinies and uprisings in many towns across Russia. All were put down, and the Ohkrana hounded many young rebels into exile.

One of the many thousands who were banished from Russia as a result of their political activities was Vladimir Ulyanov, a communist who adopted the name of Lenin in 1900. Under this name, he wrote articles attacking the Tsar and calling for an alliance of peasants and industrial workers to overthrow him.

The Creation of Communist Russia

The end of Tsarist Russia came in 1917. It was not the actions of Lenin or other radicals which brought it down. Rather it was the disasters that had befallen Russia in the First World War, when they fought with the British and the French against Germany. By April 1917 four million Russians had been killed at the front, and those left behind faced terrible hardship as the economy collapsed. Nicholas and his family were arrested.

Lenin seized the opportunity to return, and, six months after the downfall of the Tsar, his supporters ousted the new government formed by the Minister of War, Alexander Kerensky. Lenin took Russia out of the war, granting a great deal of land to Germany. Together with his friend, Leon Trotsky, who raised a new army, he set about creating a new, Communist Russia, renamed the Union of Soviet Socialist Republics.

Peter
the Great

Great in stature as well as reputation, Tsar Peter towered over most of his subjects. He ruled Russia from 1689 to 1725, transforming it from an inward-looking, background nation to a major European power. On the way, he created an army and a navy and built a splendid new capital city in the middle of a marsh. He could be cruel in support of his dream—his own son was tortured to death because he did not share Peter's vision of the new Russia—but he balanced this with an enormous energy, an inquiring mind and an adventurous spirit.

Moody, brilliant and eccentric, Peter the Great was impatient with the traditions of his people.

Peter's father, Tsar Alexis, was a religious, serious man who presided over a backward country that held him in awe. He married Peter's mother, Natalya, after his first wife died leaving two sickly heirs, Fedor and Ivan. From the Kremlin, Tsar Alexis administered his vast country through prayer and privilege. It was a haphazard way to run a state and inefficiency and corruption were part of the tradition. The social struc-

Personal Profile

PETER ALEXEEVICH – PETER THE GREAT
Born *May 30, 1672 (new style June 9)*
Died *January 28, 1725 (new style February 8)*
Parents *Alexis Mikhailovich, Tsar of Russia and Natalya Kirillovna Naryshkina, Tsarina (his father's second wife).*
Reign *1682–1725.*
Appearance *Exceptionally tall, nearly 7ft (over 2m), with dark red hair and black eyes. As a youth he was of outstanding beauty, despite a marked nervous twitching in his face.*
Personality *General liveliness, curiosity and impatience; a total lack of vanity combined with a tremendous pride; frequently drunk; intelligent but coarse; hot-tempered; a lover of practical jokes; a man of extraordinary, haphazard and restless energy.*

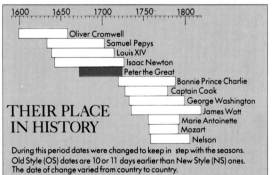

THEIR PLACE IN HISTORY

Oliver Cromwell
Samuel Pepys
Louis XIV
Isaac Newton
Peter the Great
Bonnie Prince Charlie
Captain Cook
George Washington
James Watt
Marie Antoinette
Mozart
Nelson

During this period dates were changed to keep in step with the seasons. Old Style (OS) dates are 10 or 11 days earlier than New Style (NS) ones. The date of change varied from country to country.

Peter's father, Tsar Alexis Mikhailovich, (left) ruled from 1645-1676. He was known as the "gentle Tsar", because of his kindness and humanity. Peter's half-sister Sophia Alexeevna (right), ruled as regent over her brothers. She was a fiercely ambitious and intelligent woman.

ture was closed and narrow, and Russians were suspicious of foreigners and made them live in an enclosed part of Moscow called "The German Suburb".

In 1676 Alexis suddenly died and Fedor became Tsar. When Fedor died six years later, 10-year-old Peter was proclaimed Tsar but Sophia, Peter's half-sister, organized a coup with the help of the Streltsy.

The Streltsy had been formed 100 years before by Ivan the Terrible and served as the palace guard. Membership of the Streltsy became a privilege and Sophia used their fear of change to provoke a violent attack against Peter and his family. Peter and his half-brother Ivan were then made co-Tsars, with Sophia as regent. Not surprisingly, Peter never trusted the Streltsy again and never felt at ease in the gloomy labyrinth of the Kremlin. Later, he resolved to build another modern palace and capital city, and the construction of St. Petersburg was to absorb much of his adult life.

The young Tsar was endlessly inquisitive and energetic. Later in life Peter would regret his lack of formal education, for as a young man his learning was largely directed by his own interests. For example, Peter was once given a sextant, a device which is used by sailors to work out their position at sea.-

In 1682 the Streltsy revolted in support of Sophia and overran the Kremlin (above). Peter saw the horrible deaths of his family and servants, and loathed the Streltsy ever after.

Peter demanded to know how it worked. No Russian at Court knew, so they had to turn to the German Suburb where they found a Dutch merchant named Timmerman. To teach Peter to use the tool, Timmerman had first to teach him geometry and arithmetic. These subjects in turn introduced the Tsar to other areas of learning and Timmerman became an important influence on Peter's life.

Menshikov (above) rose to become one of the most powerful men in Russia.

FATHER of the RUSSIAN NAVY

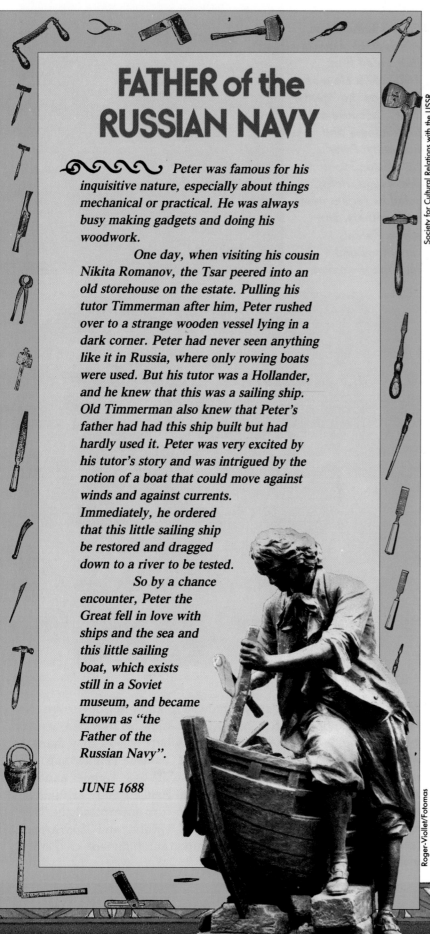

Peter was famous for his inquisitive nature, especially about things mechanical or practical. He was always busy making gadgets and doing his woodwork.

One day, when visiting his cousin Nikita Romanov, the Tsar peered into an old storehouse on the estate. Pulling his tutor Timmerman after him, Peter rushed over to a strange wooden vessel lying in a dark corner. Peter had never seen anything like it in Russia, where only rowing boats were used. But his tutor was a Hollander, and he knew that this was a sailing ship. Old Timmerman also knew that Peter's father had had this ship built but had hardly used it. Peter was very excited by his tutor's story and was intrigued by the notion of a boat that could move against winds and against currents. Immediately, he ordered that this little sailing ship be restored and dragged down to a river to be tested.

So by a chance encounter, Peter the Great fell in love with ships and the sea and this little sailing boat, which exists still in a Soviet museum, and became known as "the Father of the Russian Navy".

JUNE 1688

At 17 Peter was married to Eudoxia Lopukhina. She was devoutly religious and not well matched to her energetic husband. She bore Peter an heir, the Tsarevich Alexis, but their marriage was doomed.

Peter was effectively Tsar from 1689 when, with the help of "boyars" (Russian nobles), Sophia was overthrown and confined to a convent. For the next five years Peter indulged in one long, wild party. This involved huge drinking bouts, feasts, and extravagant practical jokes.

Peter loved the company of foreigners. His great friend at this time was Francis Lefort, a Swiss adventurer. Another friend was the Scots soldier, a former Jacobite, General Patrick Gordon who did much to help organize the new Russian army.

Peter determined to go abroad to satisfy his curiosity about other countries. With a traveling court he left Russia on what was called "The Great Embassy" to the West. Peter traveled in disguise, calling himself Peter Mikhailovich to avoid the pomp and ceremony he knew would be due to a visiting head of state. However, as he was an extremely large man, over nearly 7ft (over 2 meters) tall, Peter's presence was soon the best known secret wherever he went.

Peter's curiosity was allowed full reign. He worked as a shipwright in Holland, learned watchmaking and iron smelting in London (where he also learnt to drink much ale!). But Peter had to cut short his travels because the Streltsy had revolted again. He

In 1698, the Streltsy rebelled. Peter crushed the revolt, punishing thousands with great cruelty (left). From an early age, Peter played war games. Supplied with "troops", he planned "campaigns" using real equipment and uniforms (right).

Novosti

Moscow State Historical Museum

hurried back to Russia where he showed no mercy to the hated palace guard.

Peter disliked the ceremonial role of a monarch but was absolute in his belief of his right to rule. He could be charming and informal but he was ruthless when crossed. Peter had a violent temper, and now his rage was terrible. He was personally involved in the trial, torture and execution of thousands

of Streltsy. The cruelty of the Russian penal system which involved the use of the knout (a short whip), the rack, the wheel and public beheading gave an outlet to the darker side of Peter's nature.

Through his other great friend, Prince Menshikov, he met and fell in love with a low-born Lithuanian girl, Catherine, whom he later married. Catherine was often the

English nobles visit Deptford Dockyard (below) to peer at the Tsar of Russia who, dressed as a laborer, is learning the crafts of carpentry and shipbuilding.

PORTRAIT

Robert Harding

Peter's second wife, Catherine (above), became Empress of Russia in 1724 and ruled after his death in 1725.

Society for Cultural Relations with the USSR

Peter had a bitter and unhappy relationship with his son Alexis (left). As he considered Alexis unfit to succeed as Tsar, he condemned him to death for rejecting his father's desire to reform Russia into a modern state.

only person who could reach him when he was in one of his furious rages. She was a clever woman who understood Peter and his changeable moods. Once a courtier was wrongly accused of corruption. Peter became furious and forbade anyone, even Catherine, to talk to him about the affair. Catherine composed a petition signed in the name of Peter's favorite dog, Lisette, and attached it to the dog's collar. When the Tsar saw the petition delivered in this original manner, he laughed and granted a pardon to the unfortunate courtier. It is thought that Peter's irrational behavior may have been due to a mild form of epilepsy: it was noted that his face would twitch and sometimes his arm would shake.

Not even Catherine could mend the rift between Peter and his son, the Tsarevich, however. Alexis was deeply religious and felt that Peter's reforms were heretical. At first Peter tried to reason with Alexis. He then pleaded, but to no avail. Finally, Peter ordered his son to change his ways. Alexis fled the country but Peter dragged him back from hiding in Austria. He was arrested and died under torture. Europe was horrified at this murder, but Peter did not care. He preferred to have no heir rather than let Alexis rule his "new" Russia.

Peter's energy and curiosity lasted all his life. Once established in his new capital of St. Petersburg he had a hand in everything.

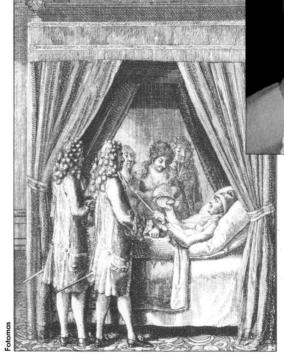

Fotomas

He would order a carriage and rush off to a foundry to beat the hot metal, then he might inspect the shipyards, witness the demonstration of a telescope or spend a few hours working on his private lathe. Even on his deathbed he issued decrees.

His energy was legendary and it was no exaggeration when a peasant remarked: "That was a Tsar, what a Tsar! He did not eat his bread for nothing, but worked like a peasant."

John Massey Stewart

In the autumn of 1724, Peter fell seriously ill from kidney stones and a bladder infection. He took to his bed in early 1725, and on January 28, in much pain, he died aged 53. Catherine never left his bedside throughout the ordeal. On his deathbed (left), he named Catherine to be his successor. Peter's death-mask (above), a cast taken from his face, is kept in the Hermitage Museum in Leningrad.

Window on the West

Peter was a dynamic but tyrannical leader who forced reform on an unwilling and barbaric Russia.

Mary Evans

Patrick Gordon (above) helped to build the army.

The Russians proclaimed their Tsar "Peter the Great, Emperor of all Russia" after his complete victory over the Swedes in 1721 which established Russia as a formidable power in the West. When Peter first came to the throne, domination by Russia's powerful neighbors — Sweden, Poland, Turkey and China — was a real threat. Peter spent his life making the changes necessary for Russia's survival, and turned a backward nation into a European power within 20 years.

His lively intelligence quickly realized the value of a modern military organization, but Peter knew that for the army to improve, the entire system that supported it had to change. But despite being absolute ruler of his country, Peter faced formidable opposition in his attempts to modernize Russia. This was largely because the country was under the control of the Russian church.

Russians rejected many of the reforms and inventions that were familiar to the rest of Europe, because they believed they were the work of "heretics", or people who were not in the Orthodox Russian Church, and many Russians considered Peter to be the Antichrist bringing ruin to Russia.

Peter decided that his people would learn from the West and employed hundreds of European experts to supervise the modernization of the state. These Europeans had the use of unlimited labor in the serfs and Peter

Peter longed for a navy and a seaport. His first ships (left) were built to fight the Turks for the port of Azov on the Black Sea and he later fought Charles XII of Sweden (right) for an outlet on the Baltic.

Giancarlo Costa

revoked all the old laws that restricted foreigners. Their religious freedom was guaranteed, they could travel where they wanted and they didn't have to pay taxes. In return they were expected to pass on their skills and knowledge to the Russians.

The boyars, the most educated people, were used to an indolent life supported by millions of serfs whom they owned and taxed. So Peter had to force them to change.

Orthodox Russians considered their beards to be a symbol of their religious belief and self respect. They were, they believed, an ornament given by God; yet Peter considered them unnecessary and uncivilized, a symbol of all he intended to change. The day after his return from the Great Embassy to Europe, he was welcomed by the leading boyars eager to show their loyalty.

Suddenly Peter produced a pair of scissors and began cutting their beards.

Peter also started more significant changes. Boyars' sons were sent to schools in France, Holland and England and the heads of noble families were made, by Imperial decree, to be involved with industry. However, this wasn't enough and Peter had to look outside his ruling class for allies in his reform program. Peter promoted people of merit, not only those of noble birth. Prince Menshikov, for example, rose from being a pastry cook's helper to become the second most important man in Russia.

Peter's improvements saw some results when he successfully seized the port of Azov from the Turks in 1696. But his failure to secure any allies against the Ottoman

TRANSPORT-RUSSIAN STYLE

The Russians developed a wide variety of sleighs to cope with their bitter winters, especially in Siberia. Some sleighs were houses with doors and windows, stocked with food for long treks. Others transported goods, with covers and roofs for protection. These were all horse-drawn but some sleighs, used to carry logs or small children, were made so that people could haul them over the snow.

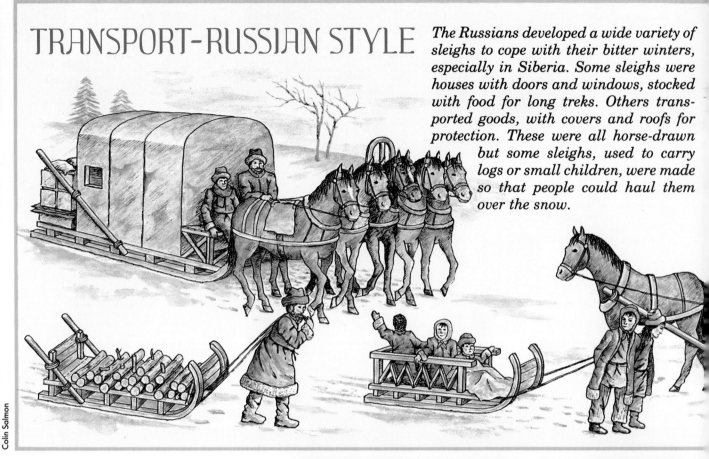

Colin Salmon

Empire forced Peter to look elsewhere for a port and access to Western markets.

Sweden was at the height of its power during Peter's time. It had taken the Baltic States of Livonia, Estonia and Ingria from Russia over 50 years before. Nonetheless, Peter still considered these states Russian by right and resolved to retake them. Unfortunately for Russia, Sweden was ruled by King Charles XII, a brilliant warrior leading a superbly disciplined nation of a million and half people. Yet, by 1703, despite a succession of humiliating defeats, Peter had secured a tiny village on the mouth of the River Neva. To the horror of his generals and the amusement of his enemies, he began to build a city on the marshy estuary.

The 21 years of the Great Northern War against Sweden were a burden on both countries, but throughout all peace negotiations Peter refused to give up this hard-won, misty, damp plot and the mouth of the Neva was transformed into St. Petersburg.

Lauros-Giraudon

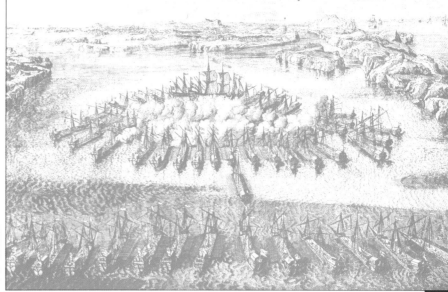

Peter proved the worth of his navy when he defeated the Swedes in the great sea Battle of Hangud (above). The Tsar's cruel use of the peasants as forced labor (below) helped push Russia into a new era of progress.

On his second trip to Europe, Peter shocked courtiers with his informality, as when he lifted young Louis XV of France (left) off his feet. The Mint in London (below) inspired Peter to introduce money to a puzzled Russia who did not know what coins were.

Peter's phenomenal energy saw him push through many changes. Peter standardized the Russian alphabet and the first books — on geometry and navigation, reflecting Peter's practical nature — were published. Many of Peter's reforms, however, failed because of the sheer backwardness of his people. He introduced a stable currency using a mint imported from London, but the people were so unfamiliar with a proper coinage that it was years before the ruble was used as everyday currency.

Even more unpopular with the boyars than industry was the navy, which did not exist before 1693, when the first keel was laid at Archangel in the north. Peter knew that Russia could never be a great power without a navy. He modernized Russia to produce an efficient army, which was able to defend a navigable seaport, in order that Russia could become a naval power and trade on its vast natural resources. He knew that access to the West was a vital element in his reform of Russia.

In order to achieve his aim to put Russia on the European stage, Peter stripped the Orthodox Church of its political power, although it retained its great influence among the people. He tortured opponents and murdered his son. He worked thousands of serfs to death building St. Petersburg, forming the navy, digging canals and working in the new mines. It is no surprise then, that his last wish as he lay dying in the capital he built was, "Protect the foreigners."

CITY OF CONTRASTS

Foreign devils and trips abroad! A young girl is amazed by the daring society of St. Petersburg.

"God and the Tsar knows," said Papa as he tried to comfort my mother. He always says that when the Tsar does something he doesn't really agree with. You see my brother, Alexander, is leaving for London in England tomorrow morning. When he told the family at supper last week, Mama was horrified. "Why, oh why does it have to be my little Alexa?" she wailed.

His Majesty has constantly disrupted our lives. We lived in Moscow until we were ordered to St. Petersburg. Papa made us turn and look at Moscow from Sparrow Hill just before sundown. We could clearly see the wonderful bell tower of Ivan the Great. As the sun went down it seemed to strike every golden roof and the whole city was glittering. When we got to St. Petersburg, surrounded by wet marshes, flat fields and cloaked in damp mist from the River Neva, I too felt sad at leaving our familiar city.

We've been here six years now, and I must say that the Tsar has made quite a city for us. Alexander said that foreigners called it the "Venice of the North". I didn't know where Venice was then. But now I'm 16 I know better. I learnt about Venice at one of the Assemblies, or court parties.

The Assemblies were a great shock to Mama. She dreaded that I would meet foreigners and immediately called Father Flotsky. As Secretary to President Yavorsky, the head of the Holy Governing Synod, the Holy Father is familiar with the customs of court life. He said he attended these parties and Mama was mollified. Then she discovered that I was expected to wear a gown without a head-dress or any covering on my arms — just gloves! Even Papa was shocked, just as he was when the Tsar ordered his beard to be cut off.

Mama took me to the lovely Church of the Holy Trinity (it's the family's favorite because it is made of wood, like churches in Moscow), where she talked to Father Flotsky and said that she had heard people call the Tsar the "Antichrist." She was careful to cross herself and then they spoke privately, while I observed my hundred protestations in honor of the Archangel Michael.

Anyway, Papa bought me a lovely blue gown and Mama made me a long shawl to go over my head and arms. Mama kept crossing herself and muttering right up until the carriage came to fetch us for the party.

To get to the Assembly we had to take the ferry. It's terrifying because the River Neva has a powerful current. The ferries have sails but rely mostly on long poles which the

FLASH BACK

ST PETERSBURG

Peter designed an elegant European city but the nation resented it. After the 1917 Revolution, the people returned to Moscow as the true capital of Russia.

Tsar Peter chose to build his capital city on the remote, marshy Baltic coast (right) far from the heart of Old Russia and the oriental splendor of the Kremlin. The city emblem (below) of St. Petersburg.

SCR Library

The Winter Palace (right), home to the tsars and of historic importance to the 1917 Revolution is now the Hermitage Museum. Peter built a lovely city designed around canals (below).

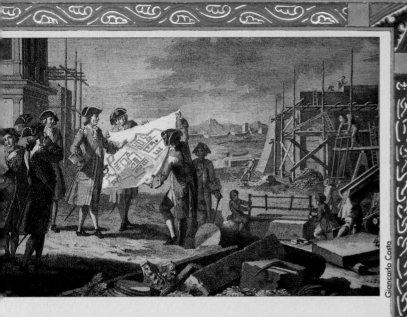

**later generation denied
eter as founder of his city** **(above) and changed its
name to Leningrad.**

**The classical arch on Palace
Square (above) and the statue
of Peter (below) are both
reminders of the great Tsar and
his role in Russian life.**

sailors dig into the river bed and then push.

Another carriage picked us up and we drove through the huge site of the canal building. There were many people milling about the precariously erected shacks that house the serfs who do the digging. There were people outside the taverns drinking and dancing, and some of them weren't wearing any clothes! Papa drew the curtains quickly and said nothing. I learnt later at the Assembly that some people get so drunk that they sell the clothes they're wearing to get another drink.

At first the Assembly was bewildering. People talked to each other, even without an introduction. The men played cards and smoked. Some people spoke French!

One of Papa's friends arrived with his two daughters. Alexander started telling them how wonderful the ferry ride had been. He has a wonderful way of telling a story and we were all captivated. Then I noticed that everyone in the room was listening. I turned around and there was the Tsar! He was standing there with his cheek resting against the palm of his hand. He was dressed in his three-cornered hat of the Preobrazhensky regiment and an old great-coat with the pockets stuffed with paper. I noticed his shoes were scuffed and his stockings had been darned even more than Papa's. I was too shocked to do anything but Alexander bowed low and Papa stepped forward and said, "My Great Lord, Tsar and Grand Duke Peter Mikhailovich, Emperor of all . . ." but the Tsar waved him silent and walked through the huge doors to the games room and everyone started talking again.

We've been to many Assemblies since then. Mama was elated that Alexander made such an impression on the Tsar. We were all sure that he would soon be given a position in the government, but when the order came sending Alexander to England to learn sailing and shipbuilding, Mama couldn't understand it. Of course, it was Alexander's story about the exciting ferry-boat trip that had attracted the Tsar, who loves the sea and has built a great navy. Mama worried that Alexander would go to hell if he mixed with foreigners. They don't observe the feast days, worship the saints or have any icons. Father Flotsky visited us and warned Alexander about the foreigners and their devil's influences. Alexander bowed 40 times to our Icon of the Blessed Virgin and we say prayers for his soul every day.

But Alexander is fit to burst with excitement. I can't wait to get his first letter. Papa is sad but service to the Tsar has its compensations because now we're rich.

Mama told me that all the money on earth can't get you into heaven. Still, it will buy me another ballgown!

Father Flotsky has come to give Alexander a last blessing. Mama says, "What use is sailing? Who wants to build ships? If foreigners are all heretics, why is our Imperial Majesty forcing us to send our son into temptation?" Father Flotsky shrugged and held her hand. Papa put his arm around her. He stood quietly for a moment and then said, "Only God and the Tsar knows."

FLASH BACK

RUSSIAN ORTHODOX CHURCH

Peter the Great wanted every aspect of Russia under his control, including the Church. Despite his, and others' attempts to crush it over the last 250 years, it survives.

Michael Holford

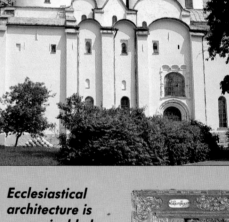

Topham Picture Library

Spectrum

The shape of this ornate crucifix with three cross bars is called the Russian cross (above).

Ecclesiastical architecture is recognizable by distinctive domes, like St. Sophia's (above). Byzantine imagery remains dominant in icons (right).

Lauros-Giraudon

Originally, wooden buildings were the norm all over Russia, like this traditional church (above). Stone could only be used for construction under royal decree and was used for grand cathedrals.

Frank Spooner Pictures

These worshipers (left) attended a special service, held in 1988, to celebrate 1000 years of the Russian Church.

Karl
Marx

orn in Germany, Karl Marx
was forced to spend much of
his life in exile because of his
political beliefs. He wandered through
Europe with his young family, settling
eventually in London, where he
researched and wrote most of the books
that made him, and his ideas, famous.
With his friend, Frederick Engels, he
produced the Communist Manifesto,
one of the most influential documents
ever written. Though he never set foot
in Russia, his political beliefs and ideas
about the way societies should be run
profoundly influenced the course of its
history.

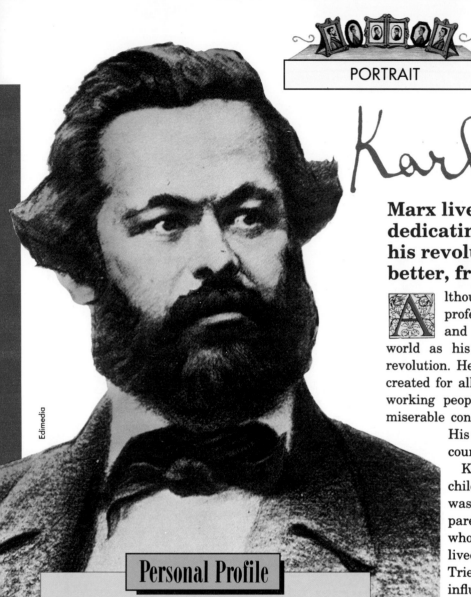

Edimedia

Karl Marx

Marx lived in poverty while dedicating his life to working out his revolutionary theories for a better, freer world.

Although Karl Marx was born into a well-off professional family, he spent his life thinking and writing about how such a comfortable world as his could be overturned by a worldwide revolution. He believed that a fairer society should be created for all, and that this could happen only when working people joined together to fight against the miserable conditions in which they lived and worked.

His ideas were to shape and change the course of history.

Karl was born in 1818, the third of nine children. After his elder brother died, Karl was the eldest boy and was doted on by his parents and sisters. His family were Jews who had converted to Christianity, and they lived in the ancient and beautiful town of Trier in Germany. Karl's father was an influential lawyer, respected for his sense of fair play.

The family had two servants, owned a hillside vineyard and had influential friends like the Baron von Westphalen, a kindly Government official who took a particular liking to young Karl. Baron von Westphalen had a daughter, Jenny, who befriended Karl. They would go for walks with the Baron over the wooded hills around Trier, when he would talk to them about great writers like Shakespeare, and problems of the day such as the growing plight of the poor.

Jenny grew into a beautiful woman, courted by many of the rich, handsome young men of Trier. But she lost her heart to Karl when he started sending her passionate love poems while at university. She called him "my darling little savage", because of his thick black beard, mop of black hair and dark, flashing eyes.

Marx began student life in Bonn by running wild. He had no interest in his subject – law – and fell into debt, spent riotous nights in taverns, and was cut over the eye when he fought a duel with another student.

Personal Profile

Born *May 5, 1818*
Died *March 14, 1883*
Parents *Heinrich Marx and Henrietta Presborck*
Personal appearance *Dark, penetrating eyes, olive skin, 5ft 6in (1.7m) tall with black, wiry hair and a full beard.*
General *An exceptionally clever child, he was the family favorite, although he had little contact with his parents as an adult. He was a man of strong feelings and had complete confidence in his own theories and ideas. He left a powerful impression, good or bad, on whomever he met. A unique political thinker, he had followers who adored him. A prolific writer of books, pamphlets and letters, he worked extremely hard for what he believed in.*

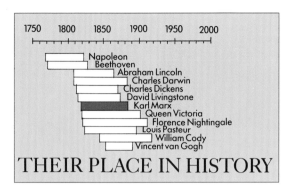

THEIR PLACE IN HISTORY

Karl's birthplace and childhood home (inset below) in Trier on the River Moselle (below). In the 19th century, the town was well known for its wine and picturesque Roman ruins.

He was then sent to university in Berlin, where he took to studying and debating history and philosophy with as much energy as he had played. It was as a student that he first met Friedrich Engels, who was to be a lifelong friend and invaluable colleague.

Marx graduated in 1841 as a Doctor of Philosophy, then began work as a journalist. His first article was a plea for press freedom. Later, his first newspaper, the *Rheinische*

Archiv für Kunst und Geschichte

At Bonn University, Karl enjoyed a boisterous lifestyle, much to his father's annoyance. He spent his free time drinking and socializing. He even fought a duel: these fights were regarded almost as sport by German students (right).

Bildarchiv Preussischer Kulturbesitz

Edimedia

After a long, secret engagement, Jenny von Westphalen (above) and Karl married in 1843.

Zeitung (Newspaper of the Rhine), was banned when it criticized the government, so Marx decided to leave Germany.

He and Jenny were married in June 1843, and, after a Swiss honeymoon, Marx found work as an editor in Paris. The French capital was alive with revolutionary ideas. These were discussed by young people yearning to make complete changes to the way society worked.

Marx joined in these discussions and often dominated them with his sharp wit and tremendous energy. He became convinced that the time was ripe for a total revolution of working people. The bosses would be thrown out, and there would be no privately owned property to cause greed and envy. People would not be divided into classes of rich and poor, but enjoy equal freedoms. These ideas were called "communism".

However, as in Germany, Marx's ideas were not welcomed by the Parisian authori-

Marx was editor-in-chief of the Rheinische Zeitung (above). This controversial paper was banned.

While studying in Berlin, Marx started reading history and philosophy. He was influenced by the work of his countryman, G.W.F. Hegel (above), whose ideal was human reason and who believed that historical progress came from conflict between old and new ideas. Marx and his friends called themselves the "Young Hegelians".

Marx would disappear into the British Museum Reading Room (above) to research the books and pamphlets he was planning to write.

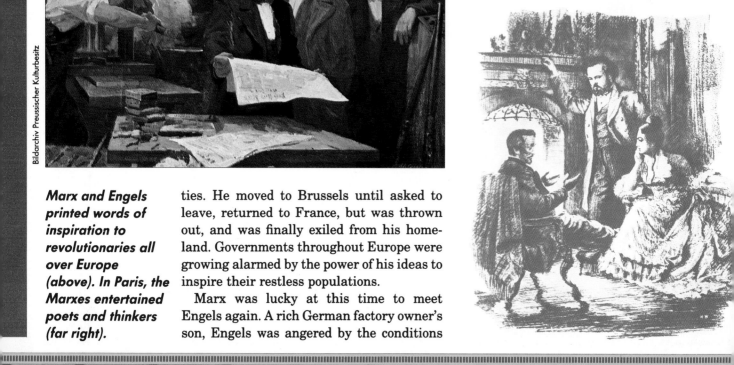

Marx and Engels printed words of inspiration to revolutionaries all over Europe (above). In Paris, the Marxes entertained poets and thinkers (far right).

ties. He moved to Brussels until asked to leave, returned to France, but was thrown out, and was finally exiled from his homeland. Governments throughout Europe were growing alarmed by the power of his ideas to inspire their restless populations.

Marx was lucky at this time to meet Engels again. A rich German factory owner's son, Engels was angered by the conditions

Above, family friend Engels (rear left) and Marx with his daughters Laura, Eleanor and Jenny (seated left to right).

Picnics on Hampstead Heath

VICTORIAN FAMILIES enjoyed special Sunday outings, and the Marx household was no exception. They loved their summer picnics on Hampstead Heath, which was then, as now, a popular park for Londoners to relax in. The walk from Soho took about an hour and a half. The girls would scamper ahead of their parents with a guest or two. Helene, the maid, followed behind, with one of the guests helping to carry a hamper filled with a cold roast and fruit.

AFTER THE MEAL, the adults read newspapers and discussed politics while the children played hide and seek. Later Marx would join in the games and give donkey rides to the children's delight. As they made their way home they would pick wild flowers, sing German songs in chorus and entertain each other reciting passages from Shakespeare.

After collaborating with Marx for almost 40 years, Engels (above) continued and translated much of his work after his death, including **Das Kapital** *(below).*

Internationaal Instituut voor Sociales Geschiedenis

AKG

Das Kapital.

Kritik der politischen Oekonomie.

Von

Karl Marx.

Erster Band.

Buch I: Der Produktionsprocess des Kapitals.

Das Recht der Uebersetzung wird vorbehalten.

Hamburg
Verlag von Otto Meissner.
1867.
New-York: L. W. Schmidt, 24 Barclay-Street.

Bildarchiv Preussischer Kulturbesitz

A servant from the age of 11, Helene Demuth (above) left Germany to join the Marx household in 1845. She cooked, cleaned and cared for the whole family and endured the years of poverty with them. She bore Marx an illegitimate son, Frederick, of whom little is known. She died in Engels' house in 1890.

her life to the family. She is buried in Highgate Cemetery in London with her master and mistress.

In 1849, when Marx was 31 years old, he at last found sanctuary in London, just as many political refugees had done. But life was hard. After a time in Chelsea, the growing family moved to Soho, into two dingy rooms which had neither toilet, nor bath, nor running water. They were always in debt, and sometimes had to sell or pawn their possessions just to survive. Because of this hardship, three of the six children died in childhood. Jenny was often ill and Marx suffered from poor eyesight, boils and other illnesses. In one of his letters to Engels, Marx wrote: "My wife is in a truly dangerous state . . . and has suffered a breakdown." But he still found time to play with his children and would let them climb on his back as he sat at his rickety desk.

Despite continual war and social unrest in Europe, the organized workers' revolt that Marx and Engels expected did not happen. However, Marx continued to believe that it would erupt in time, and to debate the issue with his fellow exiles. Inheritances from Jenny's family enabled the Marxes to move, in 1856, to a house in Hampstead, north London. But poverty continued to take its toll. Jenny died in 1881, leaving a grief-stricken Marx. Two years later, Engels and Helene found Marx dead in his armchair.

he saw when he visited Manchester on family business. People lived amid dirt and disease, and young children worked ten hours a day. Engels gave a practical edge to Marx's ideas, and continued to help Marx in every way possible – with his money, his writing and his devoted friendship.

The third member of the team was Jenny, who worked hard turning her husband's scrawls into writing the printers could understand. There was a fourth: Helene Demuth, the faithful servant who devoted

A memorial to Marx erected by the Communist Party (right). Part of the inscription reads: "The philosophers have only interpreted the world in various ways. The point however is to change it."

Bridgeman Art Library

REVOLUTION IN THE STREETS

The uprisings of 1848 threw Europe into turmoil.

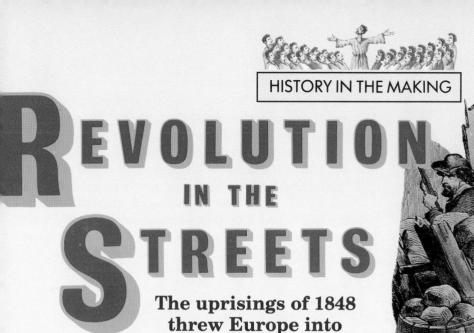

"Workers of the world unite! You have nothing to lose but your chains! You have a world to win!" With these fiery words, Karl Marx and his partner Friedrich Engels hoped to start a revolution in the restless spring of 1848.

It was a time of great unrest. In Britain, the Industrial Revolution was well advanced. At the same time, much of Europe was emerging from a feudal society in which the peasants were entirely dependent on the lord who owned the land they worked. Throughout Europe, poor harvests in the

Here the spirit of Liberty leads the people in the 1830 uprising in France.

mid-1840s meant bread (the staple diet for most people) was scarce and therefore very expensive. This led to large-scale riots, particularly in Berlin and Vienna. In France, the unpopular monarch Louis Philippe was deposed and the second Republic was proclaimed, under pressure from the people.

Marx was particularly interested in the effects of the Industrial Revolution in Britain. Here the development of machines had expanded and speeded up the production of goods. Factory owners needed workers to operate their machinery, and many out-of-work farm laborers migrated to the towns to do this. But the owners exploited them by paying low wages, while making good profits

Marx and Engels wrote the Communist Manifesto *(above) to inspire workers everywhere to unite against bad conditions (below).*

33

for themselves. Marx called this system "capitalism", and the people who owned the mills and factories "capitalists" (also called the bourgeoisie).

Capitalism, Marx believed, was doomed because the workers in the factories and mills – whom he called the "proletariat" – were beginning to see themselves as an oppressed group. Marx's studies of other philosophers had convinced him that every change in history had come when the oppressed class could no longer tolerate the conditions which were imposed on them by their

masters. He believed that this age-old struggle between the "haves" and "have nots" had reached the point of revolution. He anticipated that the workers would seize the factories for themselves, abolish all private property (one of the main ideas of communism) and share everything in a new world without rich or poor, greed or need. Only the timing of these events was uncertain.

Other European thinkers had similar ideas of social change, but they thought that it was enough for pressure to be put on mill and factory owners to improve the conditions of their workers. Marx, on the other hand, was convinced that only the determination of the most

David Cuzik

oppressed people to seize power for themselves would end the severe divisions in society. This solution he called "scientific socialism". He regarded religion as a distraction, offering false hope and consolation, and said it was "the opium of the people".

While living in Brussels, Marx joined forces with a group called the League of the Just, which had been started by some German exiles to debate the political issues of the day. The League was a secret society with code names and passwords to evade police spies. Under Marx's influence, the society changed its name to the Communist League. At a meeting held above a London pub in the winter of 1847, delegates from all over Europe pledged to work for a new society without classes or private property. They then gave Marx and Engels the task of writing a statement to tell people about their views.

The result was the *Communist Manifesto*, which was to be translated into virtually every language on earth and have as much

influence as any book since the Bible. The *Communist Manifesto* was written as a guide to action. It argued that communist society was the ideal society and would be created through the overthrow of capitalists by workers. It indicated that the ruling class (who had the power) held on to its position by the use of violence and that violence would be necessary to overcome it. It particularly condemned private ownership of factories and mills, but stated that the organized power of the working class could defeat the capitalists. "Let the ruling classes tremble at a Communist revolution", the *Manifesto* declared.

They had not long to tremble. Coincidentally, a few weeks after the *Manifesto* was published, revolutionary workers took to the streets in France, Austria, Germany and Italy and there was also unrest in Poland and Russia. "The flames are the sunrise of the proletariat," rejoiced Marx,

Manchester City Art Gallery/Bridgeman Art Library

Hoping for work in the new industries, the rural poor traveled to the towns (left).

As Marx traveled through Europe he saw chimneys filling the horizon and factories transforming the landscape. This dramatic new era was captured by artists (left and right). By the 1840s, rapid industrialization had taken place in Germany (left). The Industrial Revolution was well advanced in Britain, mainly in the north where dockyards developed and the iron and coal industries boomed (right).

Many workers, who were exploited and dissatisfied, held meetings (above) and became members of workers' associations (right) to demand change.

who arrived in Paris to find crowds singing and dancing in the streets. Yet it was a false dawn. Four days of savage street fighting broke the workers and left thousands dead.

From exile in London, Marx spent the rest of his life writing on political economy, history, science, philosophy and revolution. He continued debating with political refugees in Britain and around the world. Marx did his reading and writing in the British Museum from morning to night, working on a book called *Das Kapital (Capital)* which discusses the links between wealth and work and the way people live in a capitalist society. It took him more than 15 years to finish the first volume, and the final part of this enormous three-part work was completed by Engels. It was not published until 1894, 11 years after Marx's death.

The European uprisings of 1848 did not bring the revolutionary changes that Marx had predicted. These were to take place much later – in Russia in 1917 and in China in 1949 – both mighty revolutions inspired by his ideas.

37

CHANGING the WORLD

A waiter spies on the meetings of the Communist League, led by Marx and Engels, held in the upstairs room of a London pub.

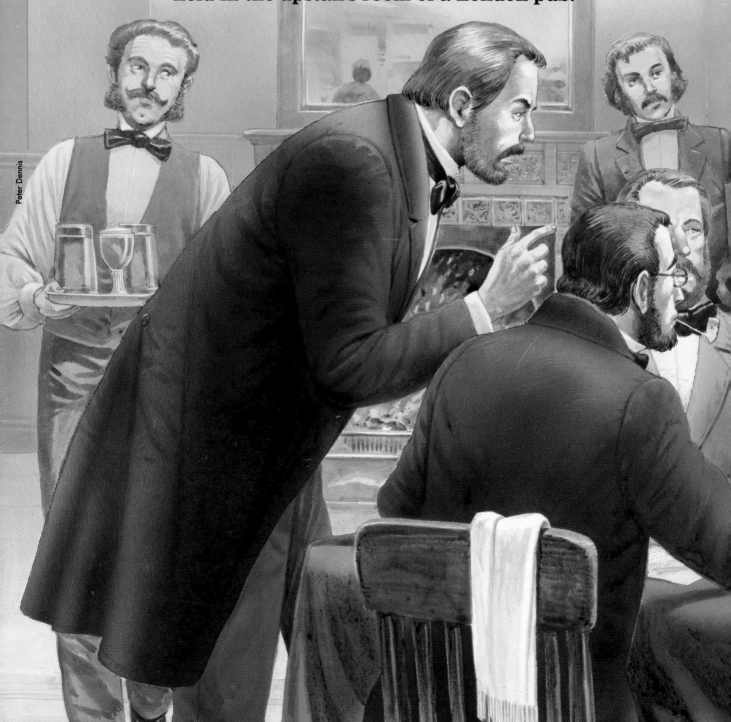

t made my hair stand on end. Here was I, in a den of foreign revolutionaries, not a hundred yards from Piccadilly and hardly a mile from the Queen herself, safe in Buckingham Palace. And on the Lord's Day, too! I wonder if they're making a special point by discussing their communist business on a Sunday night?

How many Londoners know what goes on above the Red Lion pub in Soho? Downstairs, pints of porter and other fine beers are pulled for the regulars – journeymen tailors and the like. Upstairs, it's a very different story. A poster tells you that there's a meeting of the German Workers' Educational Association, but that's not the half of it. The Educational Association is a front for the Communist League and every government on the continent of Europe would pay good money to have a spy at the keyhole up there. That's where I come in. All I have to do is keep my ears open when I take up the beers and I collect a gold sovereign from a certain Prussian gent of my acquaintance. This gent is particularly interested in what he calls "inflammatory remarks."

He told me to listen carefully for the words "Moon Calf", which he said was a code name for Queen Victoria. It seems that he had warned the British Government of a plot on the Queen's life, but was told that the police would do nothing without proof. That

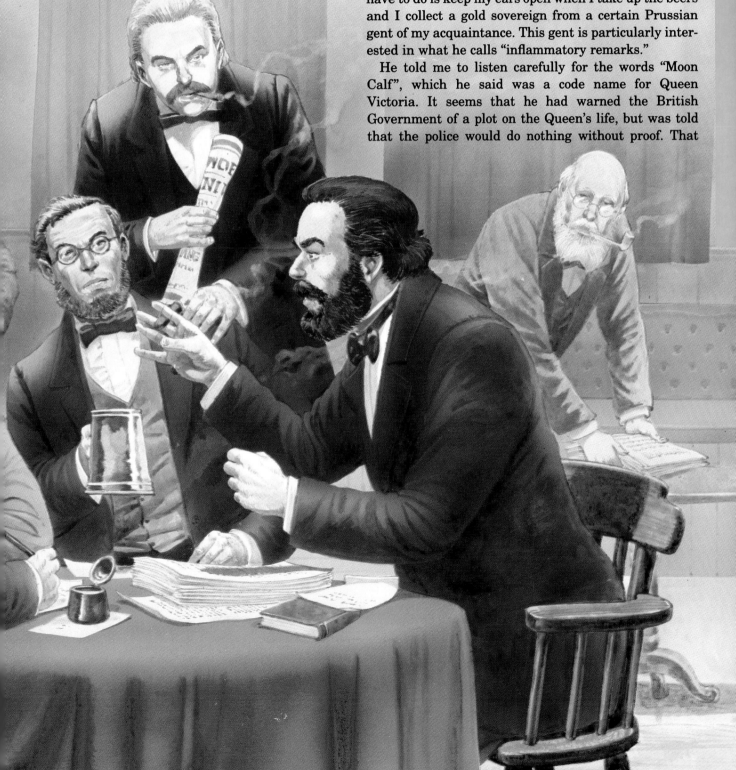

made him very angry, especially when the communists got their own back by complaining that they were being pestered by Prussian spies!

So you can imagine that I felt a bit nervous the first time the landlord of the Red Lion sent me upstairs. They were speaking German, but you could also hear some English and French too. I wasn't supposed to let on that I understood German, but when I forgot myself and answered "Ja, mein Herr" to someone wanting cheese and pickles, nobody seemed to mind and soon I got to know some of them quite well. There's Heinrich Bauer, the shoemaker, and the watchmaker Joseph Moll, whose nickname is Jupp, and Karl Schapper, who told me his father was a poor country preacher. He's got a big black mustache and has a haughty look.

The first thing that surprises you when you go up there is that there's a grand piano with some music books on it. It seems that the League began as a sort of school for working people, where they could learn to feel proud of themselves. That's what it still is in a way, because everything takes the form of instruction. On one evening, English is taught, on another geography, then history, drawing and physics, singing, dancing, and on the seventh evening, it's communist politics.

The room has tables and benches with space for up to 200 people. They begin to trickle in after work and sit down to a simple meal, or buy a penny packet of tobacco and smoke a pipe with their pot of beer in front of them. Their clothes are very respectable and they behave with a sort of quiet dignity, though you can tell that most of them are ordinary workers. By half past eight the room is full and there's a feeling of tension and excitement. When the smokers stop smoking and the room falls silent, you know the meeting's about to begin.

They call each other "Citizen" this and "Citizen" that and have long discussions about how their revolution is going to happen. It is in these discussions that Citizen Marx has come to dominate the proceedings. He's told them that the signal for liberation will come from France, because the contrast between rich and poor is greatest there. Britain, he says, is the rock upon which the sea of revolution pounds. He's not very big, but he has broad shoulders and a powerful look. His hair is as thick as a lion's mane and he looks right at you as he speaks. Everyone sits and listens intently.

His friend Citizen Engels, who is tall and as dignified as an English gentleman, usually makes a speech in which he says that everyone has to agree on one way of doing things. Then Marx takes over. His speeches are brief and he never wastes a word, but makes one point

FLASH BACK

In the 20th century, the ideas of Marx have had a tremendous influence on the politics of many different leaders and countries. From the Soviet Union to Cuba, revolutions have taken place in his name, although few have developed in the way he imagined.

Communism has had many enemies as well as followers. In the 1950s, Senator Joseph McCarthy (left) campaigned to "sweep" communism out of the U.S.A. Mao Tse-Tung (right) led the Chinese Revolution. The People's Republic of China was formed in 1949.

Macdonald/Aldus Archive

after another. Sometimes he uses a blackboard, just like a schoolmaster. Then woe betide anyone who says something he thinks stupid or wrong, like those who suggest that people will become lazy and lose their sense of freedom if they are not allowed to own personal property. His lips curl, his eyes flash and he'll jump up, bang the table, puff on his cigar and make a complete fool of the person with a few well-chosen words.

I got a few surprises when I was sent across Soho to his home to deliver some books he'd left behind. The smoky room made my eyes water and it took me a while to become accustomed to the gloom. The furniture was tattered and everything was topsy-turvy, with piles of books and papers, cracked cups, inkpots, children's toys and the children themselves all over the place.

Imagine my surprise when Marx, this wild and restless man, turned out to be so mild and gentle when among his family. He immediately offered me a pipe and tobacco and began a friendly conversation in which he asked me my opinion on politics. He spoke of his hard times since arriving in England, of the children's illnesses and lack of money, and added that sometimes he thought of emigrating to America.

He pointed out of the window at a figure with a notebook lurking in the street below and he told me that

COMMUNISM IN ACTION

One of the greatest modern playwrights, George Bernard Shaw (left) was a tireless promoter of socialist ideas throughout his long life.

Che Guevara (left) was a dashing revolutionary leader in South America. He was killed in Bolivia in 1967.

Ho Chi Minh (right), Marxist President of North Vietnam, led his country in its war against the South (backed by the U.S.A.) in the 1960s.

A selection of Marxist pamphlets (above) sold on the streets of Britain earlier this century; Fidel Castro (left) Cuba's revolutionary leader since 1959; President Mikhail Gorbachov of the Soviet Union (right), who is introducing reforms into his country.

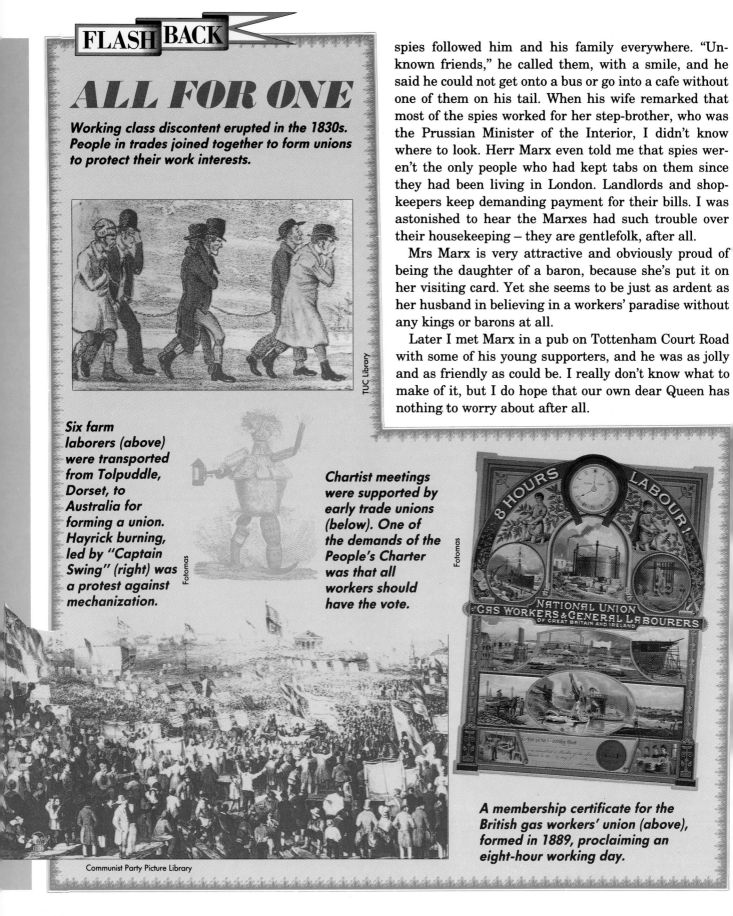

FLASH BACK

ALL FOR ONE

Working class discontent erupted in the 1830s. People in trades joined together to form unions to protect their work interests.

TUC Library

Six farm laborers (above) were transported from Tolpuddle, Dorset, to Australia for forming a union. Hayrick burning, led by "Captain Swing" (right) was a protest against mechanization.

Fotomas

Chartist meetings were supported by early trade unions (below). One of the demands of the People's Charter was that all workers should have the vote.

Fotomas

Communist Party Picture Library

spies followed him and his family everywhere. "Unknown friends," he called them, with a smile, and he said he could not get onto a bus or go into a cafe without one of them on his tail. When his wife remarked that most of the spies worked for her step-brother, who was the Prussian Minister of the Interior, I didn't know where to look. Herr Marx even told me that spies weren't the only people who had kept tabs on them since they had been living in London. Landlords and shopkeepers keep demanding payment for their bills. I was astonished to hear the Marxes had such trouble over their housekeeping – they are gentlefolk, after all.

Mrs Marx is very attractive and obviously proud of being the daughter of a baron, because she's put it on her visiting card. Yet she seems to be just as ardent as her husband in believing in a workers' paradise without any kings or barons at all.

Later I met Marx in a pub on Tottenham Court Road with some of his young supporters, and he was as jolly and as friendly as could be. I really don't know what to make of it, but I do hope that our own dear Queen has nothing to worry about after all.

NATIONAL UNION GAS WORKERS & GENERAL LABOURERS OF GREAT BRITAIN AND IRELAND

A membership certificate for the British gas workers' union (above), formed in 1889, proclaiming an eight-hour working day.

42

V.I.
Lenin

L enin came from a rebellious middle-class family—his elder brother was executed for attempting to kill the Tsar. He was exposed to the ideas of Karl Marx when he was a student, and immersed himself in political life. His activities earned him a spell in prison. In 1900 he went into voluntary exile in Germany, but continued to influence events in Russia with his writings. After the overthrow of the Tsar in 1917, he returned in triumph to oust his rivals and establish the world's first government based on communist principles.

Lenin was a committed revolutionary who became head of the world's first communist government.

The Russian Empire ruled by the Tsars was a society of extremes – poverty and hardship for many and incredible wealth in the hands of the few. Such inequalities often led to violent conflict, for the Tsarist administration was very powerful and reform was frowned upon. But this divided land was to produce a man who, through his great gifts and persistence, would change it forever.

Lenin – Vladimir Ilyich Ulyanov – was born in 1870 in the town of Simbirsk on the River Volga. Although his family continued to call him Vladimir Ilyich, Lenin was a pen-name he used from 1901 onwards, to conceal his identity from the authorities.

Lenin's family came from Russia's small professional middle class. His father was a school inspector, and his mother a doctor's daughter. They were cultured and held progressive views. At school, the young Lenin took great interest in Russian literature, history and the classics (ancient Greek and Latin). He worked hard and won the gold medal for his final exam results in 1887. However, this success was blighted by the death of his elder brother Alexander, who was executed for plotting to assassinate Tsar Alexander III.

Only 17, Lenin was deeply affected by the loss of his brother. He vowed to find another way to help the Russian people fight their way free of Tsarism.

Later in 1887, Lenin left Simbirsk and went to Kazan University to study law.

Personal Profile

LENIN (VLADIMIR ILYICH ULYANOV)
Born *April 22, 1870*
Died *January 21, 1924*
Parents *Ilya Nikolaevich Ulyanov and Maria Alexandrovna Blank*
Personal Appearance *A thin, reddish beard, high forehead and piercing brown eyes. He was almost bald by his mid-twenties.*
General *Intellectually gifted, he educated himself after being expelled from university, and read and wrote constantly. Determined to achieve his aims, he was industrious, persistent and methodical. He spent much of his life in exile in Europe with his wife; they had no children. He led the Russian Revolution, and was prepared to take "desperate measures" to defend it.*

Lenin's parents were well-educated intellectuals, photographed here (left) with their six children. In the back row, left to right, are Olga, Maria (mother), Alexander, Ilya (father), Anna. Front, Maria (on mother's lap), Dmitri and Lenin.

There he met other students who introduced him to the writings of the German revolutionary, Karl Marx (1818-83). Lenin studied Marx intensely, became very influenced by his work, and thought about how Marx's ideas could be applied to Russia. Marx's theory was that in the industrialized countries, the urban working class would overthrow the bosses who were exploiting them, and this would result in a more equal, socialist society. But in Russia, the vast majority of workers were peasant farmers. Lenin concluded that the poorer and more radical peasants could join forces with the urban work-

Baptized Vladimir, meaning "rule the world", Lenin was born in Simbirsk, in the Russian steppes (right). His family home (below) was a large wooden house with a garden, an orchard and a croquet lawn.

David Tomlinson/NHPA

SCR Library

Lenin was an avid reader. As a child, he read Tolstoy's long novel, War and Peace (right).

Kobal Collection

1850	1875	1900	1925	1950	1975	2000

Emmeline Pankhurst
David Lloyd George
Henry Ford
The Wright Brothers
Robert Falcon Scott
Mahatma Gandhi
Vladimir Ilyich Lenin
Winston Churchill
Albert Einstein
Charlie Chaplin
Martin Luther King
Neil Armstrong

THEIR PLACE IN HISTORY

St. Petersburg, later Petrograd (renamed Leningrad, above, on Lenin's death) was the scene of revolutionary unrest and victory.

Zefa

Mansell Collection

ing class to overthrow Tsarism.

By the end of 1887, Lenin was expelled from the university for his political activity. He took his exams as an external student, but still came first in the class. He began practicing law in Samara, continuing to read banned revolutionary literature. After two years, he moved to St. Petersburg, which was becoming the center of workers' unrest and opposition to the political system. Here the secret police – the Ohkrana – were vigilant in their suppression of young radicals,

Lenin saw the First World War as a struggle for power between capitalist countries, for which the working class suffered. Russian troops (above) faced appalling casualties and the lack of all essential supplies.

but Lenin still joined Marxist groups and attended illegal meetings.

The authorities had been keeping an eye on him since his brother's assassination attempt, and soon he was arrested and imprisoned for writing articles for an illegal newspaper. Lenin did exercises to keep fit in his cell, and started writing *The Development of Capitalism in Russia*. This period of imprisonment was followed by three years of exile in Siberia (north-east Russia). Here Lenin was joined by another revolutionary in exile, Nadezhda Krupskaya, whom he had met in St. Petersburg four years earlier. They were married in July 1898.

In 1900, Lenin's "internal" exile was over. Determined to remain free of the Tsar's police, he went to live in Munich. Krupskaya joined him the following year when her own term of exile ended – and so began 15 years of travel and work in different European countries. At first, Lenin's most important task was to publish a newspaper expressing Marxist views. It was called *Iskra (The Spark)* and was smuggled into Russia through a network of supporters.

While Lenin had been in exile, his political group in St. Petersburg had formed a party – The Russian Social Democratic Labor Party (RSDLP). But the party was split over policy and organization. After a vote, Lenin's

Nadezhda Krupskaya (below) met Lenin at an illegal Marxist meeting in 1894. They married four years later while in exile in a Siberian village (right).

Tass

Bryan & Cherry Alexander

Lenin planned and wrote for the revolutionary newspaper Iskra (first issue, above) meaning The Spark.

SCR Library

СКАЗКА О ЗОЛОТОМ ПЕТУШКЕ

To communicate secretly with his

Негде, в тридевятом царстве,

comrades outside St Petersburg

В тридесятом государстве,

prison, Lenin would use milk to

Жил-был славный царь Дадон.

write them invisible messages

Смолоду был грозен он

between the lines of ordinary letters

И соседям то и дело

or books. Once dry, the milk was

Наносил обиды смело,

invisible against the white page.

Но под старость захотел

The innocent-looking book or letter

Отдохнуть от ратных дел

was then sent out of prison, right

И покой себе устроить;

under the noses of the wardens. The recipients

Тут соседи беспокоить

knew they had been sent messages

Стали старого царя,

if Lenin had put a secret sign on

Страшный вред ему творя.

the book-binding or envelope. To make

Чтоб концы своих владений

the 'ink' visible, they simply

Охранять от нападений,

held the paper near a candle flame

Должен был он содержать

or immersed it briefly in hot water.

Многочисленную рать.

Moreover, as a precaution when he

Воеводы не дремали,

was writing, Lenin made 'ink-pots' of

Но никак не успевали:

bread to hold the milk; when a warder

Ждут, бывало, с юга, глядь,—

looked in on him, he popped the bread

Ан с востока лезет рать,

into his mouth. One day, he had

Справят здесь, — лихие гости

to eat six of them!

Идут от моря. Со злости

Lenin was in Geneva in 1917, when lack of food and reports of army losses led to revolt in Russia. Workers and soldiers united and the Tsar was forced to abdicate. German leaders thought Lenin could influence the Russians to stop fighting. They transported him and his companions in a sealed train, with no outside contact, to Petrograd. On his arrival, Lenin climbed onto an armored car (right) and made a stirring speech to the cheering crowd.

Jean-Loup Charmet

view prevailed and his section became known as the Bolsheviks, or majority. Lenin's aim was to lead the Bolsheviks to a revolution.

By 1905 discontent was spreading through Russia. When 200,000 workers demonstrated in St. Petersburg, the Tsar's troops fired on them. Lenin was in Geneva when he heard of this event, called "Bloody Sunday". Over the next ten years, Lenin worked to build up the strength of the Bolsheviks, both in and out of Russia. In 1917, Tsar Nicholas II was forced to abdicate and a provisional government ran the country. Lenin and the Bolsheviks gained support and, on November 6, took over Petrograd (St. Petersburg until 1914). The Revolution had succeeded and Lenin formed the world's first communist government.

Lenin never wavered from his belief that only a world guided by Marxist principles could remain free of oppression. But Bolshevik rule was not popular with everyone. As Lenin was leaving a Moscow factory in August 1918, a woman fired a gun at him. He survived this, but four years later suffered a stroke. He now worried about his successor. He warned against the leadership falling to Joseph Stalin, also in the government, as he thought him hard and unprincipled.

Lenin died, aged 53, at his home outside Moscow on January 21, 1924. The city of Petrograd was renamed Leningrad in his honour.

The Tsar, Tsarina and their five children (above) were placed under house arrest by the provisional government of 1917. After Lenin came to power, they were executed in 1918 – probably shot by the local guard under orders. Lenin aimed to sweep away kings, priests and capitalists (right).

Тов. Ленин ОЧИЩАЕТ землю от нечисти.

As a revolutionary, Lenin hid his identity with false papers, but his Party card (above) is genuine.

After Lenin died, Krupskaya wrote: "Comrades, workers and peasants! Do not build memorials to him" – but a huge mausoleum was built in Moscow (below).

ГОРДОСТЬ СОВЕТСКОГО КИНО

905 год

THE RUSSIAN REVOLUTION

Within a few months in 1917, the ancient structure of Russian society was transformed for all time.

Leon Trotsky (above), second in importance to Lenin during the revolution; Kerensky (below), prime minister during 1917.

I n 1913, the Romanov dynasty represented by Tsar Nicholas II celebrated its 300-year rule over Russia. Four years later, Romanov rule came to an end and power passed to the people.

In the first years of the 20th century, the Russian economy expanded rapidly, but not as fast as that of the more industrialized countries of Western Europe. Russian labor was mainly unskilled and desperately poor, and industrial workers made up only a sixth of the overall population.

Most Russians were peasants. Until 1861, they had been serfs: landless laborers owned by the state or the wealthy. When they were freed, a few peasants borrowed money to buy land and became burdened with debt. The others had too little land to keep them and faced starvation when the harvest failed. The death rate was high.

The terrible conditions of both urban workers and peasants sparked revolution in

Most Russians under the rule of Tsar Nicholas II were peasants (left). Poverty was common, education scarce and most peasants never saw what life was like in a town or city.

SCR Library

Popperfoto

49

1905. In St. Petersburg, 200,000 workers marched to the Winter Palace to petition the Tsar, urging him "to break down the wall" between him and his people. The troops were ordered to fire on the demonstrators and they killed over a thousand, one Sunday, later named "Bloody Sunday". Peasants attacked their landlords and demonstrations spread to other towns, but eventually the unrest was stifled and the Tsar reasserted his authority.

After the defeated uprising, an uneasy peace reigned in Russia. Measures were taken to lessen the financial burden on the peasantry and to give some rights to the workers. The Tsar also conceded the right to form a

Parliament – the Duma. Then, in 1912, a wave of strikes beset the Siberian minefields and the troops massacred 170 miners. The horror of this action created further turmoil until the outbreak of the First World War, when the Russian people temporarily united against a common enemy.

Germany declared war on Russia because Russia was allied to Serbia against the threat of Austria-Hungary and Germany. But the Russian army suffered terrible losses. The war devastated the peasant economy, as most of Russia's 15 million soldiers had been taken off the land, leaving women and the old to farm. After three years of fighting, soldiers began to desert and return to their villages, even at the risk of being executed. To help morale, the Tsar became Commander-in-Chief and went to the front. Although he was greeted with enthusiasm, major losses further demoralized the soldiers.

Meanwhile, massive price rises and severe shortages of food and fuel caused anger against the government. During February 1917, there were riots in Petrograd (formerly St. Petersburg). The Tsar ordered his troops to use force on the

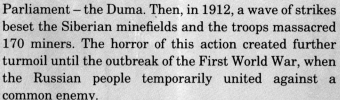

Richard Scollins

The Structure of Russian Society

This political cartoon of 1900 depicts the different levels of Russian society before the Revolution. The Tsar and the nobles are at the top, the workers and peasants at the bottom, supporting all the different classes above them. The cartoon's message could thus be understood even by those who could not read.

ROYAL FAMILY AND NOBILITY

CHURCH

ARMY

MIDDLE CLASSES

PEASANTS

summer of 1917. Disastrous defeats and loss of life led to more demonstrations against the government. The government in turn blamed the Bolsheviks for their troubles and ordered Lenin's arrest. He fled to Finland.

Kerensky appointed the authoritarian General Kornilov to restore order in the army, in early September, but Kornilov had his own plans to seize power. He advanced on Petrograd but many troops deserted and the Bolshevik Red Guard blocked him, putting a stop to his attempted overthrow of the government.

During the weeks following Kornilov's campaign, the Bolsheviks gained a tremendous amount of support, particularly within the Soviets. They set up their headquarters in Petrograd in a disused school for aristocratic young ladies, called the Smolny Institute, and there they laid their plans.

On the night of November 6, the Red Guard under Trotsky were positioned at the railway stations, telephone exchanges and banks. A red lantern was lit at the city's Peter and Paul fortress as a signal for action. When a blank shot was fired from the

protesters but they refused to do so. The Duma, in an effort to keep control, organized a provisional government under Prince Lvov. Power was no longer in the Tsar's hands and on March 15 he abdicated.

Under the provisional government, censorship was relaxed, a free press flourished and political prisoners were released. Towns all over Russia elected assemblies of workers, local councils called "Soviets" which were independent of the government.

In April 1917, Lenin returned from exile in Switzerland and enthusiastic crowds greeted the arrival of his train at the Finland Station. Lenin addressed the crowd. He told workers and peasants to seize power.

The prime minister Kerensky ordered a huge offensive against the Germans in the

52

cruiser *Aurora*, on the Neva river, the storming of the Winter Palace began.

Kerensky was in the Palace defended by some Cossack officers and a women's battalion. The fighting lasted two hours. Members of the provisional government were arrested, but Kerensky fled the city. Lenin proclaimed victory. The All Russian Congress of Soviets, controlled by the Bolsheviks, met on November 7 and declared that Soviets throughout Russia were to assume power.

Government was now in the hands of the Bolsheviks led by a 12-man Politburo and a Council of People's Commissars, of which Lenin was elected President. Lenin had promised to end the War, and on March 3 1918, he signed a peace treaty with Germany at Brest-Litovsk.

Russia lost huge areas of land through this treaty, which made the Bolsheviks unpopular. It took two years of civil war for the Bolsheviks to secure their revolution.

The Bolsheviks used posters (right) to promote their cause. A car seized by revolutionaries patrolling through Petrograd in 1917 (above).

Sent to the front line, but not required to fight, a women's battalion was formed (below). They were used to raise morale in the Tsar's army.

RASPUTIN AT COURT

A former governess of the Tsar's children tells of Rasputin's strange influence on the royal family.

My name is Madame Anya Tyutchev, former governess to the royal children, now a tired old woman. On this dark winter morning, I feel compelled to put pen to paper. For now the court favorite Rasputin is dead, surely I, more than anyone, can recount how it was that this peasant's son from Siberia could hold such power over the mightiest in Russia. I know the truth behind this mysterious story.

It was twenty years ago, in 1896, that Countess Pirakov recommended me to the Tsarina as a suitable candidate for the post of governess to her three young daughters. On our first meeting she told me what she expected of her children's governess. "Your task", she said, "is to educate the girls to love and honor their papa and prepare them to marry Europe's princes."

The first years were the happiest and there was a joyful mood throughout the palaces. In winter, we stayed in St. Petersburg and the Winter Palace seemed to vibrate with song and dance. A thousand chandeliers lit the ballroom as Russia's aristocracy enjoyed the royal entertainments. But the best times were spent in the Summer Palace at Tsarskoya Selo where there was more family life and less of the responsibilities of royalty. The children studied with me and the Tsar played cards or tennis, while the Tsarina read or walked in the grounds. She relaxed away from the city where the aristocratic ladies talked behind her back. They disliked her because she was German and asked why the Tsar had not married a Russian instead of this foreigner.

All was well until the Tsarina's fourth child, Anastasia, was born. The disappointment of not giving the Tsar a son and heir almost drove her mad. The poor woman felt as if Russia was rejecting her and she knew the women back in St. Petersburg laughed at her plight and had no sympathy.

Then in 1904, her wishes were granted and a boy, Alexei, was born. He was very weak and no-one thought he would live. He had a rare condition called hemophilia, which meant that he could not stop bleeding if he cut himself. They cosseted him and wrapped him up, even in summer, and when he could walk he was forbidden to run.

Once, when he was very ill, the doctors were preparing the Tsarina for the worst. The Tsarina's friend, Anna Vyrubova, who was comforting her, quietly sent out a messenger. An hour later a tall priest, stinking of wine and with a long ragged beard, entered the room. He went directly to the Tsarina and holding her hands in his, said to her, "Your son, little Mother, is now sleeping peacefully. He will not die."

I don't know what I thought, but the Tsar and his wife were convinced that this "holy man", Rasputin, had performed a miracle. From then on, he was a constant visitor at the court and would talk to the Tsar and Tsarina as if they were long-lost friends. "Your people love you," he told them. "I am a peasant's son and I speak for them". This must have reassured them after the people had taken to the streets to demonstrate in St. Petersburg.

However, as the months went by, rumors about Rasputin grew. Stories of his drunken

FLASH BACK

FOLK DANCE

Hulton-Deutsch

The late 19th and early 20th centuries was a golden age of Russian ballet. For the great composers who wrote the music – Tchaikovsky, Prokofiev, Rimsky-Korsakov, and Stravinsky – folk melodies from all over Russia's vast empire provided inspiration. Russian ballet companies, such as the Bolshoi, today enjoy international fame.

Piotr Ilyich Tchaikovsky (above), who wrote the music for the ballets Swan Lake, Nutcracker *and* Sleeping Beauty, *was born in 1840. His melancholy nature is often reflected in his music, which is still very popular.*

Jean-Loup Charmet

The Dance Library

Country folk of the Ukraine (above) in Western Russia, look on as a balalaika player performs and dances at the same time. Russian ballet is famous for its explosive energy, as the Kirov Company's production of Berlioz's The Corsair *(left) shows. Today, there are over 30 Russian city dance companies – many tour abroad.*

& BALLET

The survival of tradition: an Eskimo of the Soviet Far East performs a tribal dance in 1984 (above) – a ritual which has not changed for centuries.

A folk dance (above) depicted in a popular print of 1910. The man is performing the low kicking dance made famous by the Cossacks. The technical perfection of a modern ballerina: Galina Samsova in Swan Lake (right).

One of the greatest of all ballerinas, Anna Pavlova (left), toured the world in the early 1900s, and eventually formed her own company. She died in 1931.

A costume design for the dancer Vaslav Nijinsky (below) as the slave Neje in Rimsky-Korsakov's Scheherazade. A member of the company taken to Paris in 1909 by the director Diaghilev, Nijinsky brought a spirit of genius to his roles in Stravinsky's Petrouchka and The Rite of Spring. He became insane in 1917, never to recover.

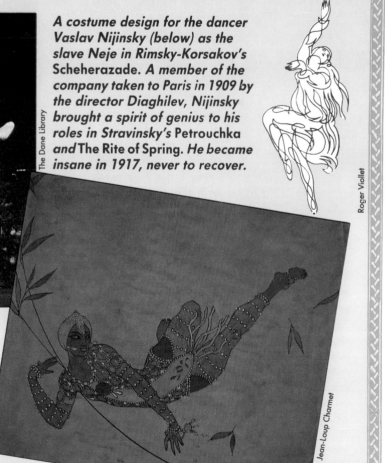

orgies and rudeness were common in the palace and many resented his influence over the Tsar. All this created a bad atmosphere.

Then the war broke out, and the Tsar went to the front as Commander-in-Chief of his forces. He left the unpopular Tsarina in charge of government, saying, "Be my ears and my eyes in the capital while I am away."

This decision proved disastrous. The Tsarina, whose mental and physical health was breaking down, was totally under the influence of the "debauched monk" Rasputin. He revelled in his power, advising the Tsarina to appoint the most unsavory characters as ministers. He even tried to dictate to the Tsar how to run the War, saying he was in direct contact with God.

As governess, I spent my evenings with the children, and Rasputin would often come into their private rooms without knocking. I did not think this was right as Olga and Tatiana were now young women. I spoke to the Tsarina about this, but she flew into a rage, said that I was mad to question the goodness of a saint, and dismissed me.

I am writing these notes, in the last month of 1916. Now that Rasputin is dead, terrible rumors about his murder are spreading through the city.

Prince Yusupov invited him to his home, offering him poisoned food and wine. Rasputin ate and drank merrily and it took three hours for the cyanide to take effect. Rasputin fell into a chair and stared at Yusupov with a penetrating glare of hatred, for by then he must have known. An hour later, he was still alive, so Yusupov fired his pistol at Rasputin, who slumped to the floor. At dawn, Yusupov returned and kneeled down to touch the body. One of Rasputin's eyes flickered open and his two powerful arms lunged out to grab his killer, who struggled free and ran upstairs in terror. Rasputin was shot again, beaten with sticks, then shoved into a car and dropped into the river – he was still breathing!

As for me, I sit here and wait, for I believe something terrible is about to happen to Russia.

FLASH BACK

Russian Fairy Tales

Fairy tales are part of traditional Russian folklore. Many have similar themes to those in the West.

A scene from the **Tale of Tsar Sultan** *(left), a poem by the Russian writer Pushkin. It recounts the journeys and adventures of the Tsar, his son and the beautiful, enchanted swan princess. The tale of the* **Wolf and the Kids** *(right), like the traditional story of the* **Three Little Pigs,** *ends with the wolf being outwitted.*

Giancarlo Costa

SCR Library

One of the famous Russian tales is **The Firebird** *(right), which tells how an archer, helped by his magical horse, accomplishes several "impossible" tasks for his king. He captures a wondrous bird, and brings back a princess from the end of the earth.*

Mary Evans Picture Library/Hodder & Stoughton

Russian fairy tales relate the timeless adventures of princesses and princes, as in the story of **Ivan and the Chestnut Horse** *(right). These stories center on a quest in which the prince overcomes evil to win the princess.*

Mary Evans Picture Library/Hodder & Stoughton

GLOSSARY

ale A type of heavy beer, flavored with hops, long a popular drink of Britain.

Antichrist An enemy of Jesus Christ, whose appearance is predicted in *I John ii 18*.

balalaika A stringed musical instrument resembling a guitar.

Bolshevik A member of the majority group in the Russian Social Democratic Labor Party; after 1918, a member of the Russian Communist Party.

boyar A landowning aristocrat in feudal Russia.

Byzantine Originating in the city of Byzantium (later known as Constantinople, now Istanbul), which was the center of the Eastern Roman Empire from 395 to 1453.

capitalism An economic system in which the means of production (mines, factories, land, etc.) are owned by private individuals who operate them for personal profit.

Chartist A supporter of Chartism, a mass movement in Britain of the 1840s in support of a People's Charter—a type of Bill of Rights.

communism An economic system in which the means of production (mines, factories, land, etc.) are communally owned by all the people—in the form of the state—and operated for the general good.

Commissar Someone in charge of a department of the government in Soviet Russia.

Cossack A member of the race of people from the south of Russia, famed for their abilities as soldiers and horsemen.

courtier A member of a monarch's court.

dynasty A family line in which power is handed down from generation to generation.

ecclesiastical Belonging to the church.

feudalism An economic system where the landowners grant others a small piece of land in exchange for part of the produce and other duties, including military service and working on the landowner's own estate.

gentlefolk People of a good or wealthy family.

heretical Against the teachings of the established church.

Hollander A native of Holland, now known as the Netherlands.

icons Religious paintings, often highly decorated, that have an important part in the ritual of the Russian Orthodox Church.

indolent Lazy, workshy.

Industrial Revolution Name given to the period (roughly 1780-1880) in which Britain was changed from a society based on farming to one based on factories.

Ivan the Terrible Ivan IV, Duke of Muscovy (the area around Moscow), who became the first Tsar of All the Russias. He earned his nickname in an orgy of cruelty and torture following the death of his wife, Anastasia, in 1557.

Jacobite A supporter of James II, King of England, after his abdication in 1688.

keel The long timber running from front to back of a wooden ship, to which all the side pieces are fixed.

Kremlin A fortified palace in Moscow, once a home of the Tsars, and now the headquarters of the Russian government.

lathe A machine which holds and turns pieces of wood so that they can be cut and shaped by an operator pressing a tool against them.

Lithuanian A native of a small state on the coast of the Baltic, for much of its history a province of the larger nations that surround it.

Manchester Industrial city in the north-west of England.

mint A place where coins are manufactured.

monarch A hereditary ruler, such as a king or emperor.

navigation The science of plotting the position and course of a boat or ship.

opium A narcotic drug derived from poppies.

Ohkrana A secret police force under the direct control of the Tsar.

Ottoman Empire An empire based in Turkey which from 1330 to 1919 ruled parts of Africa, Europe and Asia.

peasant Someone who works on the land; the word is sometimes used to refer to anyone without wealth or property in a rural area, who is also (usually) uneducated.

philosophy The study of ideas and knowledge; a search for the meaning of life.

politburo A committee of political advisers; the word comes from two Russian words meaning 'policy bureau'.

rack An instrument of torture where the victim is laid on a table and his body stretched by means of chains attached at one end to the wrists and ankles and at the other to a winding drum.

regent A person who rules on behalf of someone else who is too young or sick to look after a country by himself.

rickety Unsteady, likely to fall down.

Romanov A member of the family whose dynasty ruled Russia from 1613 to 1917.

ruble The basic unit of currency in Russia from the time of Peter the Great.

serf In feudal society, someone who was bound to work for a landowner. Although no freer to leave their masters than slaves would be, serfs were allowed to farm—but not own—a little piece of land for themselves.

smelting Heating metallic ores or rocks to obtain the pure metal.

Soho Area of London—named after a hunting cry—popular with writers, artists, and foreign exiles since the 19th century.

Soviet An assembly of workers; the basic unit of local government in communist Russia.

Tsar Ruler of Russia. The word is associated with the Latin word *Caesar* or German *Kaiser*, and literally means Emperor.

Tsarina Empress of Russia.

Tsarevich The son and heir of a ruling Tsar.

working class Those people who earn their living by hiring themselves out to others. Although it is now used mostly of those who work with their hands, Marx used it to refer to all those who did not own the means of production (land, factories, mills, etc.)

CHRONOLOGY

The Making of Modern Russia 1680 to 1926

	POLITICS AND WAR	THE ROMANOV DYNASTY
1680 to 1750	**1700-21** Great Northern War between Russia and Sweden involving other Scandinavian powers at various times. **1709** Charles XII of Sweden invades Russia, and is defeated at Poltava. **1710-11** Turkey declares war and wins back crucial port of Azov on the Black Sea **1721** Peace of Nystad. Russia takes over from Sweden as major power in the Baltic. **1733-35** War of Polish succession; Russia and Austria attempt to put a Saxon on the Polish throne. **1736-39** Russia and Austria at war with Turkey. Turks gain territory in Eastern Europe; Russia controls Azov.	**1682** Tsar Feodor dies at the age of 20, and is replaced by his brother Ivan V and half-brother, Peter I. **1689** Peter I deposes Ivan and becomes sole Tsar. **1718** Peter's son, Alexis, dies under torture. **1725** Peter dies and is succeeded by his wife, Catherine. **1727** Peter the Great's grandson becomes Tsar Peter II at the age of 11. **1730** Peter II dies. Ivan V's daughter, Anna, succeeds. Dissolute and uninterested in government, she leaves it to her lover. **1741** At Anna's death, her baby grand-nephew is proclaimed Ivan VII. A coup replaces him with Elizabeth, daughter of Peter the Great and his second wife.
1751 to 1815	**1756-63** Seven Years' War. Prussia's desire to conquer new territory is resisted by Russia, Sweden and Austria. **1762** Prussia almost beaten, but the new Tsar seeks peace. **1768-1774** War with Turkey, which gives up the Crimea. **1772** Russia, Prussia and Austria partition Poland **1787-92** War with Turkey; Russia wins Black Sea coast. **1788-90** War with Sweden. **1800-1815** Russia involved in Napoleonic wars, usually against France; gains Finland and Poland. **1812** Napoleon's army reaches Moscow before being forced to retreat by the weather.	**1762** Elizabeth dies in January. Her German-born nephew succeeds as Peter III. He is killed in July, perhaps on the orders of his wife, a minor German Princess who rules as Catherine the Great, lavishing money on the nobles at the expense of the peasants. **1796** Catherine dies of a stroke, and is succeeded by her mentally disturbed son, Paul I. **1801** Paul I is murdered by army officers and succeeded by Alexander I, known as the Golden Tsar, who leads the Russians to victory over Napoleon, forcing other European nations to recognize Russia's power.
1816 to 1865	**1827-29** War with Turkey. Russia gains territory south of the Caucasus mountains. **1833** Turkey closes the Dardanelles, the passage from the Black Sea to the Mediterranean, to non-Russian ships. **1841** European powers guarantee Turkish independence if the Dardanelles are closed to all warships. **1847** Poland becomes a province of Russia. **1853-56** Crimean War. France and England aid Turkey against Russia. At peace congress in Paris, Black Sea declared neutral, and Russia gives up territory.	**1825** Nicholas I succeeds his father as Tsar. High-handed and arrogant, Nicholas' actions lead Russia into the Crimean War, destroying much of his father's work. **1855** Nicholas's son succeeds as Alexander II. He combined liberal reforms with a hatred of those who opposed him.
1866 to 1905	**1873** Alliance of German, Russian and Austrian empires. **1877-8** War with Turkey regains Crimean War losses. **1891** Three Emperors renew alliance for 12 years. **1897** Russia occupies Port Arthur, on the Pacific coast. **1900** Russian troops occupy Manchuria. **1902** Minister of Interior Sipyagin murdered. Peasants revolt put down by new minister Plehve. **1903-5** War with Japan brings defeat; Port Arthur lost. **1904** Plehve murdered. **1905** Revolts in St. Petersburg and provinces and a naval mutiny put down with difficulty.	**1881** Alexander II assassinated by a bomb in St. Petersburg. He is succeeded by his son, Alexander III, a huge man, and like his grandfather, a believer in absolute rule. **1894** Alexander III dies at the age of 50. He is succeeded by his 26 year-old son Nicholas II, a gentle, even dreamy young man, who was destined to be the last of the Romanov Tsars. **1904** Nicholas's son, the Tsarevitch Alexei born.
1906 to 1926	**1906** General strike. First meeting of Duma. **1911** Prime Minister Stolypin murdered. **1914-18** First World War. Germany, Austria and Turkey against Russia; heavy losses lead to unrest at home. **1917** Tsar unseated. Lenin's Bolsheviks in power. **1924** New constitution renames country U.S.S.R. **1926** Stalin ousts Trotsky and becomes absolute ruler.	**1907** The monk, Grigor Rasputin, in St. Petersburg and apparently "cures" the Tsarevitch's hemophilia. **1916** Rasputin murdered. **1917** Nicholas deposed in February Revolution. Royal family arrested and kept under house arrest. **1919** Nicholas and his family murdered in Ekaterinburg.

Russia's foreign policy has been dominated by its lack of seaports. Several wars were fought with Turkey for control of lands around the Black Sea and in Eastern Europe so that Russia could gain access to the Mediterranean. At home, generations of Tsars taxed their people into poverty to pay for these wars.

RELIGION AND SOCIETY	ART AND EXPLORATION	
1698 Peter beards the boyars as a symbol of his determination to modernize Russia. 1700 Russia adopts Julian calendar. 1703 Foundation of St. Petersburg. First Russian newspaper, *Vyedomosti*, published. 1705 Moscow University founded. 1711 Administrative Senate formed. 1734 Commercial treaty with England until 1786.	1697-8 Peter the Great journeys to the West. 1716-7 Peter's second journey to the West. 1725 Vitus Bering, a Danish seaman, sent to Kamchatka by Peter the Great. He builds boats and discovers the sea passage which separates Alaska and Russia, known as the Bering Strait. 1733-41 Bering's second voyage of exploration along the Aleutian Islands and down the coast of Alaska. While he is away, others map Russia's north coast and the Arctic Ocean. 1741 Bering dies of scurvy.	1680 to 1750
1762 Peter III attempts social reforms, but is killed. 1762-96 Reign of Catherine the Great; during this time various imperial decrees made serfs of many thousands of peasants who had previously been free. 1773-5 Massive Cossack rebellion led by Emelyan Pugachev threatens Moscow. The repellion is put down. 1775 Pugachev executed. 1785 Catherine grants Charter of the Nobles, giving them exemption from taxes and direct control over the government of several provinces.	1789 Catherine the Great claims North American territories explored by Bering as part of Russia. 1799 Tsar Paul signs charter of Russian-American Company, set up to control mining and hunting on the North American mainland and to explore further south. Governor of Alaska sets up fort on Sitka Island.	1751 to 1815
1825 Army revolt fails. 1839 Child labor prohibited. 1853 Nicholas II demands protectorate over all Orthodox Christians in Turkey, the act which brought about the Crimean War. 1862 Liberation of the serfs. 1864 Provincial councils set up.	1824 Russia and U.S.A. sign Frontier Treaty. 1825 Publication of Alexander Pushkin's *Boris Godunov*. 1830 Publication of Pushkin's *Eugene Onegin*. 1835 *Dead Souls* by Nikolai Gogol, first great Russian novel, is published. 1837 Pushkin, Russia's national poet, killed in a duel. 1839 Ross Colony, southernmost Russian settlement in North American, abandoned. 1862 Publication of *Fathers and Sons* by Ivan Turgenev. 1865 Publication of Tolstoy's *War and Peace*.	1816 to 1865
1869 Abolition of the hereditary priesthood in the Orthodox Church. 1876 Foundation of Socialist People's Party. 1884 Abolition of the Poll Tax, last remnant of serfdom. 1891-1904 Building of the Trans-Siberian railway, which joins Moscow to the Pacific. 1902 Peasant's revolt put down by Minister Plehve. 1903 Russian Labor Party splits into liberal Mensheviks (minority) and radical Bolsheviks (majority). 1905 Tsar responds to unrest by issuing reform program.	1866 Dostoyevsky's *Crime and Punishment* is published. 1867 All Russian North American territories abandoned and sold to the U.S.A. for $7 million ($12.30 a square mile). 1877 Tolstoy's *Anna Karenina* completed. 1879 Peter Tchaikovsky's *Eugen Onegin* first performed. 1880 First publication of Dostoevsky's *Brothers Karamazov*. 1881 Death of Dostoevsky. 1893 Tchaikovsky's *Symphonie Pathétique* written. Tchaikovsky dies. 1902 Maxim Gorky's *Night's Lodging* published.	1866 to 1905
1906 New constitution sets up a parliament, the Duma. 1917 Effective power taken by soviets – councils – of workers, soldiers and peasants. 1918-22 Bolshevik Red Army defeats expeditionary forces sent by 12 countries to overturn the revolution. 1920-21 Drought destroys harvests; famine. 1925 Trotsky loses control of the Red Army	1907 Publication of Gorky's *Mother*. 1910 Death of Leo Tolstoy 1925 Pioneer Russian film director, Sergei Einstein, releases his classic *The Battleship Potemkin*, about the 1905 mutiny.	1906 to 1926

FURTHER READING

Almedingen, E.M. *Land of Muscovy: The History of Early Russia* (Farrar, Strauss, and Giroux, New York, 1972)

Clark, Philip *Russian Revolution* (Marshall Cavendish, New York, 1988)

Feinberg, Barbara S. *Marx and Marxism* (Franklin Watts, New York, 1985)

Finney, Susan and Patricia Kindle *Russia to the Revolution* (Good Apple, Carthage, IL, 1987)

Goldston, Robert *The Russian Revolution* (Bobbs Merrill, New York, 1966)

Halliday, E.M. *Russian Revolution* (Horizon Caravel, New York, 1967)

Hoff, Rhoda *Adventures in Eyewitness History* (Henry Z. Walck, Inc., New York, 1964)

Maclean, Fitzroy *Portrait of the Soviet Union* (Holt, New York, 1988)

Moscow, Henry *Russia Under the Czars* (Horizon Caravel, New York, 1962)

Putnam, Peter *Peter, the Revolutionary Tsar* (Harper and Row, New York, 1973)

Rawcliffe, Michael, *Lenin* (David and Charles, New York, 1989)

Resnick, Abraham *Lenin: Founder of the Soviet Union* (Childrens Press, Chicago, 1987)

Resnick, Abraham *Russia: A History to 1917* (Childrens Press, Chicago, 1983)

Ross, Stewart *The Russian Revolution: 1914-1924* (Bookwright, New York, 1989)

Stanley, Diane *Peter the Great* (Macmillan, New York, 1986)

Stein, Conrad *Siege of Leningrad* (Childrens Press, Chicago, 1983)

Stewart, Gail B. *The Soviet Union* (Crestwood House, Riverside, NJ, 1990)

Tessendorf, K.C. *Kill the Tsar! Youth and Terrorism in Old Russia* (Macmillan, New York, 1986)

Topalian Elyse, *V.I. Lenin* (Franklin Watts, New York, 1983)

Zoshchenko, M. *Lenin and the Stove Mender* (Imported Publications, Chicago, 1984)

INDEX

Michael Holford